BALLET

I0141001

Marjorie Seevers

xist Publishing

Check out all of the books in the Dancing Through Life Series

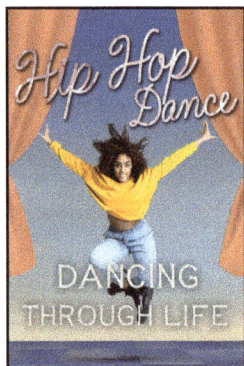

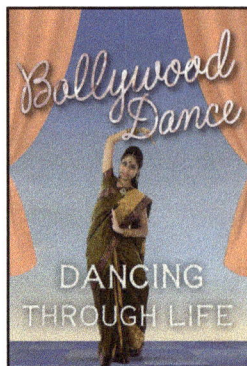

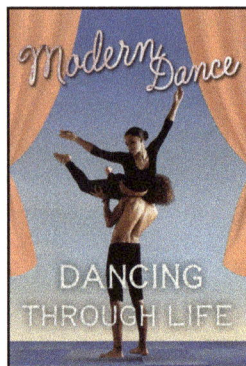

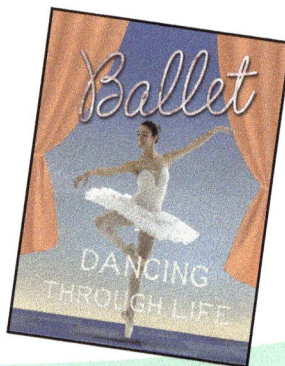

Published in the United States by Xist Publishing
www.xistpublishing.com
© 2025 Copyright Xist Publishing

First Edition
Hardcover ISBN: 978-1-5324-5437-0
Paperback ISBN: 978-1-5324-5438-7
eISBN: 978-1-5324-5436-3

PUBLISHED IN TEXAS

Contents

DANCING
THROUGH
LIFE

Chapter 1 What is Ballet?

Introduction to Ballet

Ballet is a beautiful kind of dance. It started in France over 400 years ago. Ballet mixes music, dance, and stories. The dancers do not speak. They use movements, gestures, and faces to tell the story.

Every ballet performance shares a story. Some ballets are about love and friendship. Others tell tales of adventure or magic. The dancers move in ways that match the music. This brings the story to life. Each step, jump, and spin in ballet has its own name. This makes ballet both beautiful and detailed.

Ballet spread from France to other parts of the world. Now, people everywhere love and perform ballet. Ballet dancers are called ballerinas. They spend many years practicing to get better. They need to be strong, graceful, and focused. Watching a ballet is like seeing a painting move. Each show is full of skill, emotion, and beauty.

In ballet, the dancers often wear special costumes that fit the story they are telling. The sets, lights, and music all work together to make a magical experience for the audience. Whether the story is about magical forests, royal palaces, or far-off places, ballet invites you to step into a world full of wonder and imagination.

History of Ballet: From France to the World

Ballet started in the royal courts of France over 400 years ago. It was made to entertain kings, queens, and their guests. The first ballets were performed in large, fancy halls. Dancers wore beautiful costumes and moved gracefully to tell stories without words.

As time went on, ballet became more popular. It spread from France to other countries in Europe. Italy, Russia, and England became known for their ballet performances. Each country added its own style and traditions to ballet. This made ballet more interesting and unique.

In Russia, ballet became very popular. Russian dancers trained hard and learned new techniques. They made ballet more challenging and exciting. Many famous ballets, like Swan Lake and The Nutcracker, were created in Russia. These ballets are still performed all over the world today.

Ballet also came to America. American dancers and choreographers brought new ideas to ballet. They mixed ballet with other dance styles, like jazz and modern dance. This created new and exciting performances that people loved.

Today, ballet is performed and enjoyed all over the world. Dancers from many different countries train to be the best they can be. Ballet schools and companies teach the art of ballet to new dancers. Each dancer brings their own culture and style to the stage, making ballet a truly global art form.

Ballet's journey from France to the world shows how dance can connect people from different places. It brings together different cultures, ideas, and traditions. Ballet keeps growing and changing, but its grace and beauty stay the same.

Chapter 2: Meet the Ballerina

Who Can Be a Ballerina?

Anyone can be a ballerina. Boys and girls both dance ballet. It doesn't matter where you are from or how old you are. If you love to dance and are willing to work hard, you can be a ballerina.

Ballerinas come in all shapes and sizes. What matters most is their love for dance and their dedication to practicing. Ballet takes time and effort to learn. Dancers must practice every day to improve their skills. This practice helps them become strong, flexible, and graceful.

When starting ballet, dancers learn the basic steps and positions.
As they get better, they move on to more difficult moves. Some ballerinas dream of dancing in big shows. Others just enjoy dancing for fun. No matter their goal, all ballerinas share a love for ballet.

The Different Roles in Ballet

In ballet, there are many different roles that dancers can play. Some roles are big, and some are small, but all are important to the story.

One of the main roles in ballet is the prima ballerina. She is the lead dancer in the performance. The prima ballerina often dances the most challenging and beautiful parts. She tells the main story through her dance. Everyone watches her closely as she moves gracefully across the stage.

There is also a male lead dancer, called the danseur. He often dances with the prima ballerina. Together, they perform amazing lifts and spins. The danseur shows strength and control in his movements.

Other dancers play roles like fairies, animals, or even magical creatures. These roles help to tell the story and add excitement to the performance. Each dancer must work as part of a team. They must dance in time with the music and each other.

Corps de ballet is the name for the group of dancers who perform together. They move as one, creating beautiful patterns on the stage. Even though they do not have the lead roles, they are very important. The corps de ballet makes the show come alive.

In every ballet, each dancer has a role that adds to the whole performance. Whether they are a lead dancer or part of the corps de ballet, every role is special and helps tell the story.

Chapter 3: Ballet Basics

First Steps: Positions and Movements

Ballet is built on a strong foundation of basic steps and positions. These basics are the first things every dancer learns when they start ballet. Mastering these moves takes time and practice, but they are the building blocks for everything else in ballet.

The first thing a dancer learns is the positions of the feet. There are five main positions, each with a different way to place your feet. These positions help dancers keep their balance and move smoothly from one step to another. Learning these positions is like learning the ABCs of ballet.

Next, dancers learn how to plie. A plie is when a dancer bends their knees while keeping their feet flat on the ground. This move helps to warm up the legs and make them stronger. It also helps dancers to jump higher and land softly.

Another important move is the tendu. In a tendu, the dancer slides one foot along the floor, pointing their toes. This move makes the legs and feet stronger and more flexible. It also looks very elegant.

As dancers get better, they learn to jump and spin. A jump in ballet is called a sauté. Dancers must push off the ground with their feet and land softly. Spinning is called a pirouette. To do a pirouette, a dancer must turn on one foot while keeping their body balanced.

These basic steps and positions are the start of every ballet. They help dancers move gracefully and tell the story with their bodies. Even the most advanced dancers practice these basics every day. They are the foundation of every beautiful ballet performance.

Ballet Positions

1 2 3 4 5

Plie

Tendu

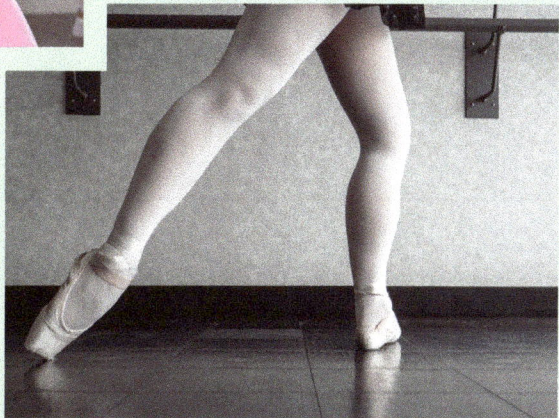

Sauté

Relevé

Arabesque

Understanding Ballet Terms

Now that you know some steps, let's learn about movements. These movements help dancers connect steps and move across the stage. Each movement is done with grace and care.

One common movement in ballet is the relevé. In a relevé, dancers rise up on their toes. They lift their heels off the ground. This movement makes dancers look taller and more elegant. Relevé is used before spins or jumps. It gives dancers extra height and control.

Another important movement is the arabesque. In an arabesque, a dancer stands on one leg. They stretch the other leg straight behind them. The arms are extended, one in front and one to the side. The arabesque shows a dancer's balance and flexibility. It is one of the most beautiful poses in ballet.

Ballet also includes flowing movements like the port de bras. Port de bras means "carriage of the arms." It describes how dancers move their arms from one position to another. The arms move softly, like floating through the air. Port de bras expresses emotion and adds beauty.

To travel across the stage, dancers use chassé. In a chassé, one foot chases the other. The dancer glides forward or backward. This movement is light and quick, like a playful chase. Chassé helps dancers move with speed.

Another movement is the glissade. In a glissade, the dancer slides one foot to the side. Then, they bring the other foot to meet it. This movement is smooth and close to the ground. Glissade links steps together, making the dance look seamless.

These movements, along with the basic steps, form ballet's language. Dancers use them to create patterns and tell stories. With practice, these movements become second nature. They allow dancers to perform with grace and confidence.

Chapter 4: Dressing for Ballet

The Ballet Outfit:
Leotards, Tights, and Tutus

Ballet dancers wear special outfits for practice and performances. These clothes help them move freely and look graceful. The main parts of a ballet outfit are the leotard, tights, and tutu.

The leotard is a tight top that covers the body. It allows dancers to move their arms and legs easily. Leotards come in many colors and styles. Some have long sleeves, while others have short or no sleeves. The leotard shows the lines of the body. This helps the teacher see if the dancer is doing the steps correctly.

Tights are worn under the leotard. They cover the legs and make them look smooth and neat. Tights also keep the muscles warm. This helps prevent injuries. Ballet tights are usually pink or white, but they come in other colors too. They fit tightly to the legs, just like the leotard fits tightly to the body.

The tutu is a special skirt worn over the leotard. Tutus are made of light, fluffy fabric like tulle. They come in different lengths and shapes. Some tutus are short and stick out. Others are long and flowy. The tutu adds a touch of magic to a dancer's outfit. It makes them look like they are floating on air.

Together, the leotard, tights, and tutu create the classic ballet look. These clothes are not just beautiful. They also help dancers perform their best. Each piece of the outfit is designed to make the dancer feel comfortable and confident on stage.

Leotard

Tutu

Tights

Flat Shoes

Pointe Shoes

Ballet Shoes – Pointe vs. Flat Shoes

Ballet dancers wear special shoes to help them move gracefully. There are two main types of ballet shoes: flat shoes and pointe shoes. Each type has a different purpose.

Flat shoes are the first ballet shoes a dancer wears. They are soft and flexible, so dancers can feel the floor. Flat shoes help dancers learn basic steps and positions. The shoes fit snugly to the foot, allowing easy movement. Flat shoes have thin soles and are usually made of leather or canvas. Both beginners and experienced dancers wear flat shoes during practice.

Pointe shoes are for more advanced dancers. These shoes have a hard, flat tip for standing on the toes. This is called dancing "en pointe." Pointe shoes are made with layers of fabric, glue, and satin. They give strong support to the feet and ankles. Wearing pointe shoes requires a lot of strength and training. Dancers usually wear them after many years of practice in flat shoes.

Flat shoes are comfortable and easy to move in. They are perfect for learning and practicing ballet steps. Pointe shoes are more challenging to wear. They allow dancers to perform harder moves that look light and airy. Both types of shoes are important in a dancer's journey.

Dancers take good care of their ballet shoes. Flat shoes may wear out and need replacing often. Pointe shoes, because they are more delicate, also wear out quickly. But each pair helps dancers improve and reach new levels in ballet.

Chapter 5: The Big Performance

Preparing for the Stage

Preparing for a ballet performance takes a lot of work. Dancers must be ready both physically and mentally. The preparation begins long before the day of the show.

First, dancers practice their routines over and over. They learn every step, turn, and jump until they can do them perfectly. This practice helps build confidence. Dancers often rehearse for many hours each day. They work hard to make sure everything looks smooth and graceful.

Next, dancers must prepare their costumes and shoes. Each costume must fit perfectly. Dancers try on their costumes and make sure they can move easily in them. They also check their shoes to ensure they are in good condition. If a shoe is worn out, it must be replaced.

On the day of the performance, dancers arrive at the theater early. They need time to warm up their muscles. Warming up is very important to avoid injury. Dancers stretch and do exercises to get their bodies ready.

After warming up, dancers put on their costumes and makeup. Makeup is used to make their faces look bright and expressive under the stage lights. Hair is styled neatly, often in a bun, to keep it out of the way during the dance.

Before going on stage, dancers practice one last time. This final rehearsal helps them feel prepared. They go over the most difficult parts of the dance. Then, they take a moment to relax and focus. Dancers often take deep breaths to calm their nerves.

When everything is ready, the dancers wait backstage. They listen for their cue to go on stage. Each dancer feels a mix of excitement and nervousness. But they are ready to give their best performance.

The Joy of Performing Ballet

Performing ballet on stage is a special experience. After all the hard work and preparation, it's time for the dancers to shine. The joy of performing ballet comes from sharing their passion with the audience.

When the music starts, dancers feel the excitement. They move gracefully, telling the story with their bodies. Each step, turn, and jump is done with care. The dancers feel proud of what they have learned and practiced.

As they dance, the audience watches closely. The lights are bright, and the stage feels magical. Dancers connect with the music and the audience. They express emotions like happiness, sadness, or excitement through their movements. The joy of dancing comes from this connection.

Applause from the audience makes the dancers feel appreciated. It shows that their hard work has paid off. Each clap is a sign that the audience enjoyed the performance. This makes the dancers feel happy and proud.

Performing ballet also brings joy because it's a chance to work with others. Ballet is often a team effort. Dancers support each other on stage. They move together, making the performance beautiful. This teamwork is a big part of what makes performing ballet so special.

The joy of performing ballet stays with the dancers even after the show ends. They feel a sense of accomplishment. They know they have done their best and shared something beautiful. This feeling encourages them to keep dancing and improving.

For dancers, the stage is a place of happiness and expression. The joy of performing ballet is something they carry with them in every step they take.

Conclusion

Ballet is more than just a dance. It's a way to tell stories and express emotions. Ballet helps people connect with others. From learning steps to performing, ballet teaches hard work and discipline. Each move is a step toward becoming a better dancer.

Ballet requires dedication and passion. Whether you dream of being a professional or just enjoy dancing, ballet offers something special. It teaches grace, strength, and the joy of movement.

Anyone can be a ballerina if they work hard. Whether you are in flat shoes or en pointe, each moment in ballet is a chance to grow. The joy of ballet is in every practice and every lesson.

So, keep dancing and keep learning. Most importantly, keep enjoying the magic of ballet. Your journey as a dancer is just beginning. There is so much more to discover. Ballet will always be there to inspire you and bring joy.

Glossary

Arabesque: A ballet pose where a dancer stands on one leg with the other leg extended straight behind them.

Ballerina: A female ballet dancer.

Chassé: A movement where one foot chases the other across the floor, often used to travel forward or backward.

Corps de ballet: The group of dancers who perform together, creating patterns and supporting the main dancers.

Danseur: A male ballet dancer, often the partner to the prima ballerina.

Glissade: A sliding movement where one foot moves to the side and the other foot follows, keeping the motion smooth and close to the ground.

Leotard: A tight-fitting garment worn by dancers, covering the body but leaving the legs free.

Pirouette: A spin on one foot, requiring balance and control.

Plie: A movement where a dancer bends their knees while keeping their feet flat on the ground, used to warm up and strengthen the legs.

Port de bras: The movement and positioning of the arms in ballet, used to express emotion and add beauty to the dance.

Prima ballerina: The lead female dancer in a ballet performance.

Pointe shoes: Special ballet shoes with a hard, flat tip, allowing dancers to perform on the tips of their toes.

Relevé: A movement where a dancer rises onto the balls of their feet or onto their toes, often used before spins or jumps.

Sauté: A jump in ballet, where dancers push off the ground with their feet and land softly.

Tendu: A movement where a dancer stretches one foot along the floor, pointing the toes to strengthen the legs and feet.

Tutu: A light, fluffy skirt worn by ballet dancers, often made of tulle, that adds to the magical appearance of the costume.

Index

www.ingramcontent.com/pod-product-compliance
Lightning Source LLC
LaVergne TN
LVHW070834080426
835508LV00027B/3445